IDENTIFY TREES AND SHRUBS BY THEIR LEAVES

A GUIDE TO TREES AND SHRUBS NATIVE TO THE NORTHEAST

Edward Knobel

Revised by

E. S. Harrar
James B. Duke Professor of Wood Science
School of Forestry, Duke University

DOVER PUBLICATIONS, INC., NEW YORK

To find the name of a tree or shrub. Choose a few leaves from the middle of a branch; leaves on young shoots are often deformed.

1. Observe if the leaf is:

(a) *Feather shaped* (pinnate); *i. e.*, composed of 3 or more leaflets on the main leafstalk, like the rays on a feather.

(b) *Hand shaped* (palmate); *i. e.*, the main veins spreading from the end of the leafstalk like the fingers of a hand.

(c) *Simple; i. e.*, of one piece which may be divided, lobed, or cut up in various ways.

2. Observe if the leaves grow:

(a) *Opposite* each other, in 3's or in clusters.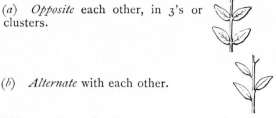

(b) *Alternate* with each other.

This may be easily observed on young shoots.

Published in Canada by General Publishing Company, Ltd., 30 Lesmill Road, Don Mills, Toronto, Ontario.
Published in the United Kingdom by Constable and Company, Ltd., 10 Orange Street, London WC 2.

This Dover edition, first published in 1972, is an unabridged republication of the work originally published by Bradlee Whidden in 1894 under the title *A Guide to Find the Names of All Wild-Growing Trees and Shrubs of New England by Their Leaves*. A new descriptive list of the species has been prepared especially for this edition by Professor E. S. Harrar.

International Standard Book Number: 0-486-22896-7
Library of Congress Catalog Card Number: 72-85500

Manufactured in the United States of America
Dover Publications, Inc.
180 Varick Street
New York, N. Y. 10014

3. Observe if the edge of the leaf is:

(*a*) *Double sawtoothed.*

(*b*) *Single sawtoothed or toothed.*

(*c*) *Wavy or smooth.*

4. Observe if the general shape of leaf is:

(*a*) *Pear shaped* (obovate) ; *i. e.*, the upper half wider than lower half.

(*b*) *Oval ; i. e.*, both halves about equal.

(*c*) *Egg shaped* (ovate); *i. e.*, the lower half wider than upper half.

A drawing of the leaf and a number referring to description may be found if the leaf is :

(*a*) *Feather shaped* and *alternate*, on plates I., II., or III.

    ,,   ,,   ,, *opposite*, on plate IV., in clusters, II., 16.

(*b*) *Hand shaped* and *alternate*, on plate V. or VI.

    ,,   ,, *opposite*, on plates VI., XII., 144, 145.

(*c*) *Simple, alternate,* and *cut up, divided,* or *lobed,* on plates VI., VII., VIII.

    ,,   ,,   ,, *double sawtoothed*, on plates VIII., IX., XII., 134.

    ,,   ,,   ,, *wavy sawtoothed*, on plates VII., XII., 138.

NOTE. If several leaves similar to the one under examination be found in the plate, read the key to that plate which gives the distinctive marks of difference.
Compare main ribs and veins of leaf with the drawing.
Illustration 119 appears almost opposite, though it grows alternate.

(*c*) *Simple*, *alternate*, and *sawtoothed*, and round, long stemmed, on plate X.

,, ,, ,, ,, ,, long and narrow, on plate X.

,, ,, ,, ,, ,, oval, on plates VIII., 64, 68, IX., 77, XI., XII.

,, ,, ,, ,, the teeth small and indistinct, on plates X., XIII.

·, ,, ,, *smooth*, on plates XIII., X., 94, 95, 107, 108, 109, XI., 122, 125, 130, XIV., 193.

,, *opposite*, and *sawtoothed*, on plate XII.

,, ,, ,, *smooth*, on plate XIV.

(*d*) *Needle shaped* (like the spruce and the pine), on plate XV.

Plate I. Nut Trees.

(*a*) 5 to 9 leaflets.	Side leaflets not symmetrical on the leaf stalk.	5 leaflets; first 3 much larger than last 2; middle leaflet *pear shaped*, *fine* sawtoothed	1
		Middle leaflet *oval*, *dull* sawtoothed . . .	2
	Side leaflets symmetrical on leaf stalk.	Middle leaflet on short footstalk	3
		Middle leaflet, no footstalk	4
(*b*) Many leaflets.	Not symmetrical on footstalk		5
	Symmetrical on footstalk		6

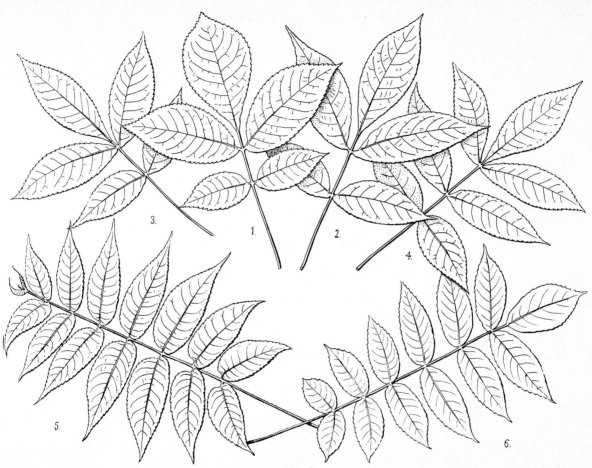

3.

1.

2.

4.

5.

6.

Plate I.

Plate II.

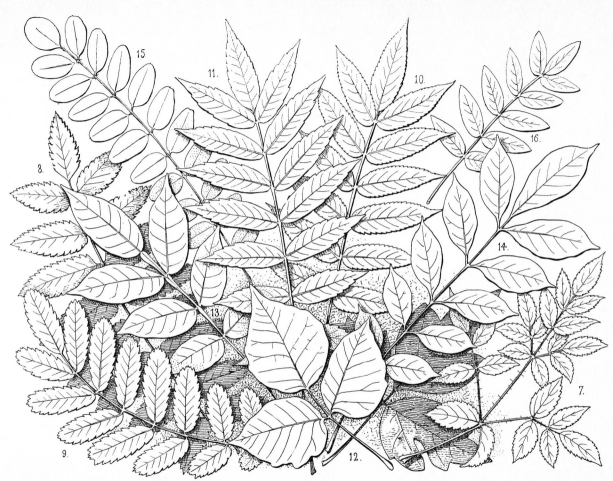

Plate II.

Plate III. Blackberry, Raspberry, and Roses.

Leaflets pointed; 3 or 5 on young shoots.

White underneath.
- Weak prickles; if 5 leaflets, the last 2 the largest . . . 17
- Stout thorny; if 5 leaflets, the last 2 the smallest . . . 18

Green both sides.
- No prickles, middle leaflet diamond shaped 19
- Stout thorns, rough woolly . . 20
- Weak prickles, smooth trailing, 21

Leaflets blunt.
- 3 leaflets, evergreen, trailing, *blunt* sawtoothed 22

5 or more leaflets.
- *Weak prickles, sharp* sawtoothed 23
- *Stout thorns,* sharp sawtoothed 24

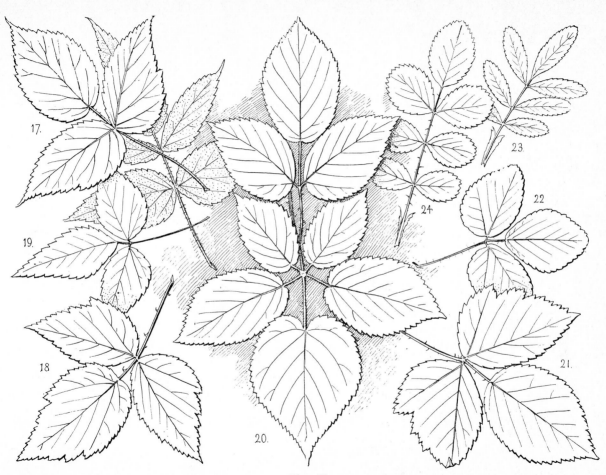

Plate III.

Plate IV.

Plate IV.

Plate V.

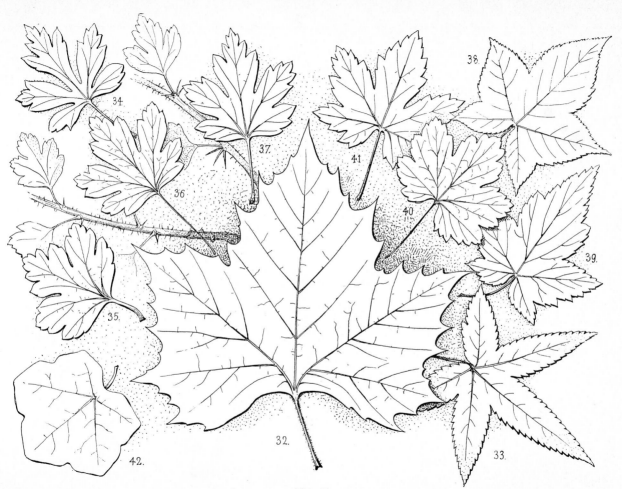

34.
36.
35.
37.
41.
38.
40.
39.
32.
42.
33.

Plate V.

Plate VI.

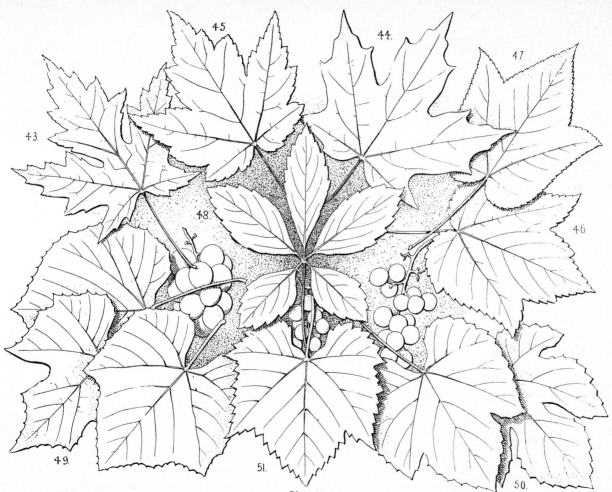

Plate VI.

Plate VII. Oaks.

Plate VII.

Plate VIII.

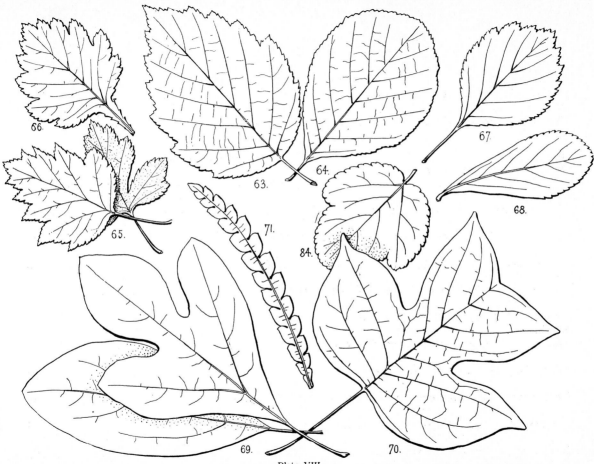

Plate VIII.

Plate IX.

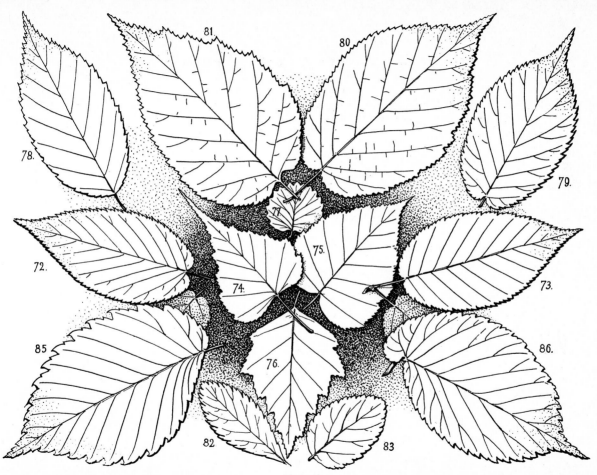

Plate IX.

Plate X. Poplars and Willows.

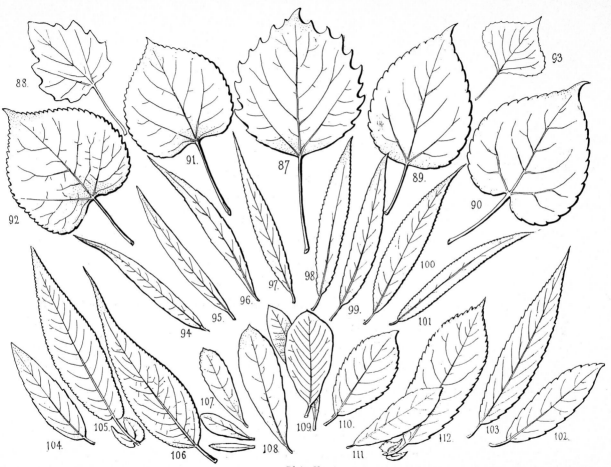

Plate X.

Plate XI.

24

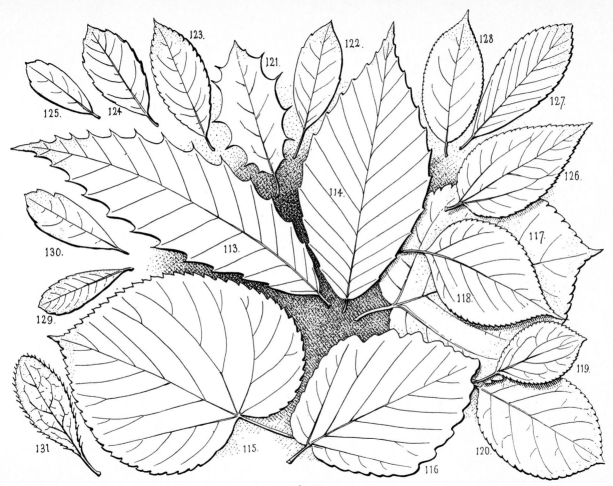

Plate XI.

Plate XII.

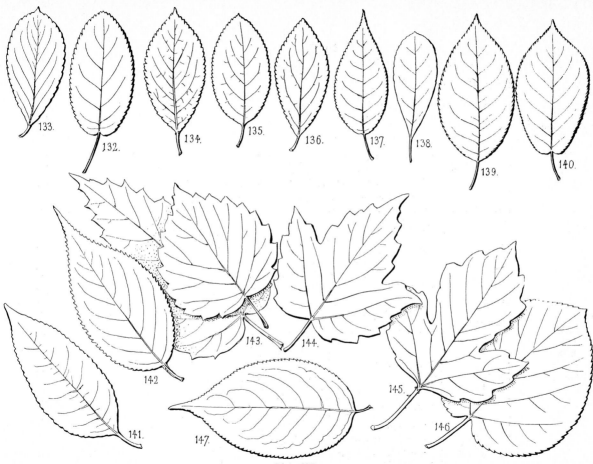

133. 132. 134. 135. 136. 137. 138. 139. 140.

141. 142. 143. 144. 145. 146. 147.

Plate XII.

Plate XIII.

Climbing vines, not evergreen, heart shaped. { Thorny 148
Not thorny 149

TRAILING
CREEPING
EVERGREEN.
- Toothed. { Pear shaped 181
  Egg shaped 182
- Pear shaped. { Very short leafstalk 180
  Leaf narrow, longer leafstalk, trailing 185
- Oval. { Round, both ends 187
  Pointed both ends 183
- Round, long stalk 184
- Heart shaped, no stalk 186

LOW
BUSHES.
- Pear shaped.
  - Pointed. { Leaf small and narrow, no stalk 161
    Leaf larger, on leafstalk 164
  - Rounded. { With short point, edge smooth 166
    No point, upper half wavy, evergreen 177
- Egg shaped.
  - Small and narrow. { Pointed 160
    Blunt, evergreen 179
  - Small, heart shaped, evergreen 176
  - Edge smooth 167
  - Fine, sawtoothed 163
- Oval.
  - Not evergreen.
    - Pointed. { Edge smooth 164
      Edge slightly toothed on sides 162
    - Blunt and opposite. { Leaves in 3's, stalked 172
      No stalk 173
  - Evergreen. { Very narrow and small, pointed 178
    Rounded both ends 175
    Hairy on leafstalk 174

Leaves scalelike, clasping the stem 168

SHRUBS AND
TREES.
- Evergreen. { Pear shaped, long stalk, pointed 171
  Oval, short stalk, pointed 170
  Oval, very short stalk, blunt 169
- Oval.
  - Very short leafstalk. { Rounded sawteeth 158
    Indistinctly toothed on sides 157
    Fine, hairy, toothed 159
    Edge smooth 159
    Wavy, woolly underneath 159
    No leafstalk, stem jointed, edge smooth 156
  - Longer leafstalk. { Long and blunt 153
    Rounded at leafstalk, tree 150
    Pointed or narrowed in leafstalk, tree 151
- Pear shaped.
  - Rounded point 165
  - Long and narrow, hairy on edge. { Smooth 154
    Downy below 155
  - Broad, limbs grow horizontal, tree 151
  - Broad, aromatic odor, a shrub 152

28

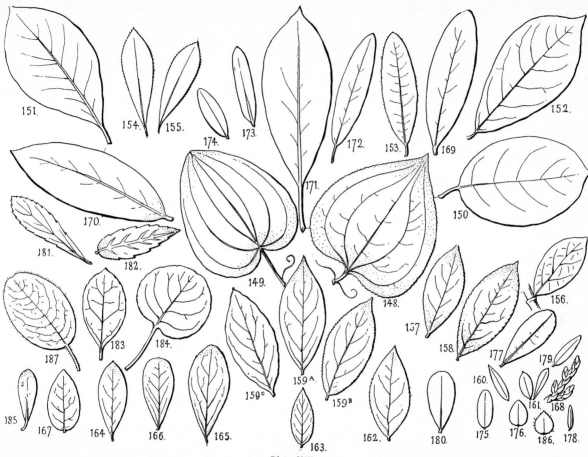

Plate XIII.

Plate XIV.

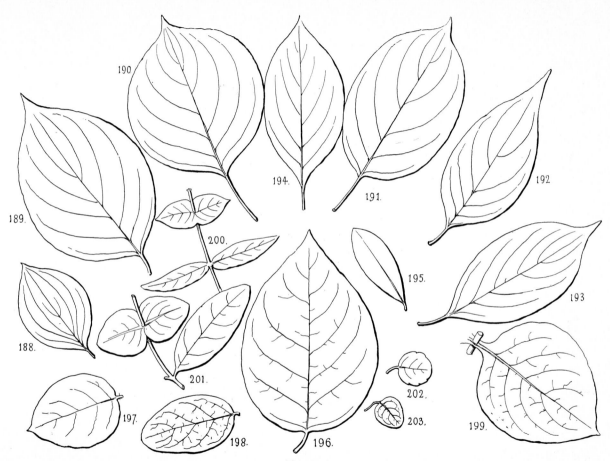

189.

190.

194.

191.

192.

200.

195.

193.

188.

201.

197.

198.

196.

202.

203.

199.

Plate XIV.

Plate XV. Needle Woods.

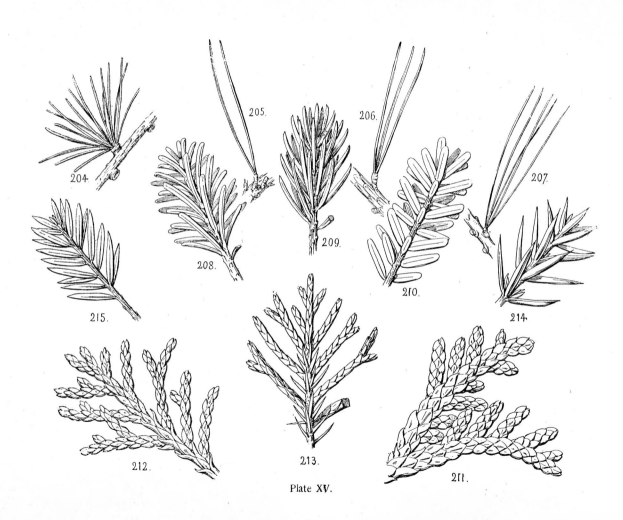

204.

205.

206.

207.

208.

209.

210.

215.

212.

213.

211.

214.

Plate **XV.**

1. **Shagbark Hickory.** *Carya ovata.* Tree, 80 ft. Bark shaggy; nut enclosed in a thick, 4-parted husk; seed sweet.

2. **Pignut Hickory.** *Carya glabra.* Tree, 70 ft. Bark with rounded interlacing ridges and deep fissures; nut pear-shaped, enclosed in a thin, tardily dehiscent husk; seed bitter.

3. **Mockernut Hickory.** *Carya tomentosa.* Tree, 70 ft. Bark firm, with low, rounded, interlacing ridges and shallow fissures; nut thick-shelled; seed sweet; leaves aromatic.

4. **Bitternut Hickory.** *Carya cordiformis.* Tree, 70 ft. Bark smooth or shallowly furrowed; nut globular; seed bitter.

5. **Black Walnut.** *Juglans nigra.* Tree, 90 ft. Bark divided by deep furrows into anastomosing ridges; nut globular, the shell corrugated; seed sweet; pith chambered, pale yellow.

6. **Butternut.** *Juglans cinerea.* Tree, 50 ft. Bark divided into flat ridges; nut oblong, with glandular husk and corrugated shell; seed sweet and oily; pith chambered, black.

7. **Bristly Sarsaparilla.** *Aralia hispida.* Shrublike, 2 ft. Only the aromatic spicy rootstalk woody; fruit berrylike, borne in clusters.

8. **American Mountain-Ash.** *Sorbus americana.* Shrub or slender tree, 20 ft. Blossoms white, in flat clusters; berries bright orange-red.

9. **European Mountain-Ash.** *Sorbus aucuparia.* Tree, 30 ft. Berries bright red, about twice as large as those above.

10. **Staghorn Sumac.** *Rhus typhina.* Tree, 20 ft. Fruit scarlet, flowers yellowish-green; young shoots covered with woolly hairs.

11. **Smooth Sumac.** *Rhus glabra.* Shrub, 10 ft. Yellowish-green scented flowers, fruit velvety crimson, shoots smooth.

12. **Poison-Ivy.** *Toxicodendron radicans.* Creeping and climbing; flowers yellowish-white; berrylike fruits white; poisonous to touch.

13. **Shining Sumac.** *Rhus copallina.* Shrub, 6 ft. Branches and footstalks dotted with raised, rusty-brown lenticels; berries crimson.

14. **Poison-Sumac.** *Toxicodendron vernix.* Shrub, 15 ft. Stem gray, young shoots purplish. Our most poisonous plant.

15. **Black Locust.** *Robinia pseudoacacia.* Tree, 30 ft. Flowers yellowish-white, in chains, pleasantly scented, fruit a small legume; twigs armed with spines.

16. **Prickly Ash.** *Zanthoxylum americanum.* Shrub, 5 ft. Stem gray, shoots brown, wood yellow, bark bitter.

17. **Wild Red Raspberry.** *Rubus aculeatissimus.* Shrub, 4 ft. Flowers white, berries light red and edible.

18. **Blackcap Raspberry.** *Rubus occidentalis.* Shrub, 3 ft. Flowers white, berries purplish-black and edible.

19. **Dwarf Raspberry.** *Rubus triflorus.* Shrub, 1 ft. Fruit red, juicy, acidulous.

20. **Thornless Blackberry.** *Rubus canadensis.* Shrub, 6 ft. Berries black, large; ripening in late summer.

21. **Low Blackberry.** *Rubus villosus.* Trailing. Berries, black, large and sweet, ripening in the early summer.

22. **Swamp Blackberry.** *Rubus hispidus.* Trailing. Berries red or purple, sour.

23. **Virginia Rose.** *Rosa virginiana.* Shrub, 2 ft. Flower rose color, fruit smooth.

24. **Carolina Rose.** *Rosa carolina.* Shrub, 7 ft. Flower rose color, fruit bristly.

25. **Virgin's Bower.** *Clematis virginiana.* Climbing. Flowers white; the small dry fruits subtended by long featherlike structures.

26. **American Bladdernut.** *Staphylea trifolia.* Shrub, 10 ft. Fruit a more or less persistent, 2 or 3 lobed, papery, bladderlike sac containing 2 or 3 shining brown seeds.

27. **Red Elder.** *Sambucus racemosa.* Shrub, 6 ft. Flowers white, berries red.

28. **American Elder.** *Sambucus canadensis.* Shrub, 10 ft. Flowers white, fruit purplish-black.

29. **Black Ash.** *Fraxinus nigra.* Tree, 70 ft. Slender, dark granite-gray bark; twigs yellowish with lighter dots.

30. **Green Ash.** *Fraxinus pennsylvanica.* Tree, 50 ft. Dark ashy-gray bark.

31. **White Ash.** *Fraxinus americana.* Tree, 70 ft. Whitish bark; twigs gray-green with gray dots.

32. **American Sycamore.** *Platanus occidentalis.* Tree, 100 ft. Bark thin, exfoliating to reveal white inner layers; the small hairy-tufted fruits borne in ball-like clusters.

33. **Sweetgum.** *Liquidambar styraciflua.* Tree, 40 ft. Gray bark with corky ridges on the branches; leaves fragrant when bruised; the small podlike fruits borne in ball-like clusters.

34. **Swamp Black Currant.** *Ribes lacustre.* Berries small, dark purple, and bristly.

35. **Roundleaf Gooseberry.** *Ribes rotundifolium.* Berries small, purple, smooth and sweet.

36. **Hairystem Gooseberry.** *Ribes hirtellum.* Shrub, 3 ft. Berries small, purple, sweet and smooth.

37. **Pasture Gooseberry.** *Ribes cynosbati.* Shrub, 3 ft. Berries large, covered with long prickles.

38. **Purple-Flowering Raspberry.** *Rubus odoratum.* Shrub, 5 ft. Flowers large, purple-rose color; small reddish fruits not palatable.

39. **Black Currant.** *Ribes floridium.* Shrub, 4 ft. Flowers large, berries black.

40. **Red Currant.** *Ribes vulgare.* Shrub, 3 ft. Straggling; fruit red and smooth.

41. **Skunk Currant.** *Ribes prostratum.* Stem low, straggling; berries red and bristly, exhaling a skunklike odor.

42. **Moonseed.** *Menispermum canadense.* Climbing vine. Flowers white; fruit black, grapelike.

43. **Silver Maple.** *Acer saccharinum.* Tree, 60 ft. Bark gray; twigs yellowish-brown to reddish-brown, exhaling a fetid odor when crushed.

44. **Sugar Maple.** *Acer saccharum.* Tree, 80 ft. Bark gray with thick plates or ridges. The sap of this tree is the source of maple syrup and maple sugar.

45. **Red Maple.** *Acer rubrum.* Tree, 40 ft. Stem gray; twigs crimson, dotted with brown.

46. **Mountain Maple.** *Acer spicatum.* Shrub, 10 ft. Bark brown with olive stripes.

47. **Striped Maple.** *Acer pensylvanicum.* Tree, 20 ft. Bark green striped with white.

48. **Virginia Creeper,** *Parthenocissus quinquefolia.* Vine. Berries upright, dark blue.

49. **Fox Grape.** *Vitis labrusca.* Vine. Grapes large, dark purple, black, or white.

50. **Summer Grape.** *Vitis aestivalis.* Vine. Grapes dark blue; ripe in October.

51. **Frost Grape.** *Vitis vulpina.* Vine. Grape dark purple, almost black; as large as a pea; acid, but good; ripens late.

52. **Post Oak.** *Quercus stellata.* Tree, 30 ft. Acorns on very short stems; small and sweet.

53. **Bur Oak.** *Quercus macrocarpa.* Tree, 40 ft. Acorns 1 in. long, deep in a mossy, fringed cup.

54. **White Oak.** *Quercus alba.* Tree, 60 ft. Acorns 1 in. long; edible, particularly when roasted.

55. **Swamp White Oak.** *Quercus bicolor.* Tree, 60 ft. Whitish shaggy bark, peeling off in shreds; many horizontal branches; acorns sweet.

56. **Chestnut Oak.** *Quercus prinus.* Tree, 50 ft. Acorn 1 in. long, sweet; bark reddish-gray.

57. **Dwarf Chinkapin Oak.** *Quercus prinoides.* Shrub, 4 ft. Our smallest oak. Acorns sweet, many on a twig; bark bitter.

58. **Chinkapin Oak.** *Quercus muehlenbergii.* Tree, 30 ft. Bark whitish, wood very yellow; acorns 3/4 in. long, sweet and edible.

59. **Scrub Oak.** *Quercus ilicifolia.* Shrub, 8 ft. Bark greenish-black, dotted with gray; acorns 1/2 in. long, bitter.

60. **Black Oak.** *Quercus velutina.* Tree, 90 ft. Under bark yellow, wood reddish; acorns 1/2 in. long, very bitter, kernel yellow.

61. **Northern Red Oak.** *Quercus rubra.* Tree, 75 ft. Bark on upper trunk dark green-gray, smooth; acorns 1 in. long, kernel white and bitter.

62. **Scarlet Oak.** *Quercus coccinea.* Tree, 70 ft. Bark reddish-gray, under bark reddish; acorns 1/2 in. long, kernel white and bitter.

63. **Speckled Alder.** *Alnus rugosa.* Shrub or tree, 20 ft. Bark reddish or dark green, with light gray dots.

64. **Hazel Alder.** *Alnus serrulata.* Shrub, 15 ft. Bark gray, with horizontal, oblong, gray-orange dots.

65. **Thicket Hawthorn.** *Crataegus intricata.* Tree, 20 ft. Flowers white, rosy tinted; fruits fleshy, bright scarlet-red.

66. **Pear Hawthorn.** *Crataegus calpodendron.* Tree, 15 ft. Fruit crimson or orange-colored, pear-shaped; edible.

67. **Dotted Hawthorn.** *Crataegus punctata.* Tree or shrub, 15 ft. Fruits dull red, yellowish with white dots.

68. **Cockspur Hawthorn.** *Crataegus crus-galli.* Tree, 20 ft. Fruits bright red; slender, long thorns.

69. **Sassafras.** *Sassafras albidum.* Tree, 30 ft. Young shoots, bright green; oval, dark blue berries, on red stems.

70. **Yellow-Poplar.** *Liriodendron tulipifera.* Tree, 100 ft. Flowers, 2 in. wide, greenish-yellow, marked with orange.

71. **Sweetfern.** *Comptonia peregrina.* Shrub, 2 ft. A round-headed bush; twigs fragrant.

72. **Sweet Birch.** *Betula lenta.* Tree, 80 ft. Bark dark purplish, smooth; leaves aromatic, spicy.

73. **Yellow Birch.** *Betula alleghaniensis.* Tree, 80 ft. Bark dirty yellowish-gray, with silvery lustre, peeling off and shaggy.

74. **Gray Birch.** *Betula populifolia.* Tree, 40 ft. Bark chalky white, with black spots.

75. **Paper Birch.** *Betula papyrifera.* Tree, 100 ft. Bark white, with pearly shine.

76. **River Birch.** *Betula nigra.* Tree, 50 ft. Bark reddish-chocolate color, ragged and broken.

77. **Dwarf Birch.** *Betula pumila.* Shrub, 2 ft. Bark brownish, dotted with warty specks.

78. **American Hornbeam.** *Carpinus caroliniana.* Tree, 20 ft. Stem fluted; bark bluish-gray, smooth; nuts 8 sided, taste like chestnuts; white, hard wood.

79. **Hophornbeam.** *Ostrya virginiana.* Tree, 40 ft. Bark brownish, finely furrowed; very hard, white wood; nut small and smooth.

80. **Common Hazel.** *Corylus americana.* Shrub, 8 ft. Fruit cover leafy.

81. **Beaked Hazel.** *Corylus rostrata.* Shrub, 6 ft. Fruit cover long-beaked and bristly.

82. **Meadow-Sweet.** *Spiraea latifolia.* Shrub, 6 ft. Flowers white; stem red-copper colored.

83. **Hardhack Spiraea.** *Spiraea tomentosa.* Shrub, 5 ft. Flowers purple-rose colored; stem dark bronze.

84. **Common Ninebark.** *Physocarpus opulifolius.* Shrub, 7 ft. Flowers white, with rosy tinge; bark usually in long shreds.

85. **American Elm.** *Ulmus americana.* Tree, 120 ft. Crown spread often 100 or more feet.

86. **Slippery Elm.** *Ulmus rubra.* Tree, 50 ft. Crown ascending; inner bark mucilagenous.

87. **Bigtooth Aspen.** *Populus grandidentata.* Tree, 50 ft. Bark light greenish-gray, smooth, leathery.

88. **Silver Poplar.** *Populus alba.* Tree, 70 ft. Bark light gray; lower surface of leaves white.

89. **Balsam Poplar.** *Populus balsamifera.* Tree, 80 ft. Bark light gray, smooth leatherlike.

90. **Balm-of-Gilead.** *Populus candicans.* Tree, 100 ft. Bark light gray; buds sticky–resinous and aromatic.

91. **Quaking Aspen.** *Populus tremuloides.* Tree, 40 ft. Bark white clay-colored, smooth, and leathery; dark brown, triangular blotches under the limbs.

92. **Eastern Cottonwood.** *Populus deltoides.* Tree, 80 ft. Bark dark gray; seed with large, white cottony tufts.

93. **Lombardy Poplar.** *Populus nigra* var. *italica.* Tree 70 ft. Bark brown-gray; branches not spreading, shape like an unopened umbrella.

94. **Basket Willow.** *Salix viminalis.* Small tree, 15 ft. Best willow for basket work; grows in wet meadows.

95. **Sage Willow.** *Salix candida.* Shrub, 5 ft. Twigs reddish; a whitish-looking bush.

96. **Longleaf Willow.** *Salix longifolia.* Tree, 20 ft. Lower stems and branches upon sweeping the ground often take root.

97. **Weeping Willow.** *Salix babylonica.* Tree, 25 ft. Branches and leaves drooping.

98. **Silkyleaf Willow.** *Salix sericea.* Shrub, 10 ft. Of grayish appearance, on sandy riverbanks.

99. **Stalked Willow.** *Salix petiolaris.* Shrub, 10 ft.

100. **Crack Willow.** *Salix fragilis.* Tree, 40 ft. Bark very rough; young shoots, smooth, polished green.

101. **Black Willow.** *Salix nigra.* Tree, 50 ft. Bark Rough; buds covered with a single caplike scale.

102. **Missouri River Willow.** *Salix eriocephala.* Shrub or small tree, 15 ft. Fruit long, silky.

103. **White Willow.** *Salix alba.* Tree, 80 ft. Young shoots bright yellow or reddish.

104. **Pussy Willow.** *Salix discolor.* Shrub, 15 ft. Grows in low meadows.

105. **Heartleaf Willows.** *Salix cordata.* Shrub or small tree, 15 ft.

106. **Shining Willow.** *Salix lucida.* Shrub or tree, 15 ft. Leaves, glossy green.

107. **Dwarf Pussy Willow.** *Salix tristis.* Shrub, 1-1/2 ft.

108. **Prairie Willow.** *Salix humilis.* Shrub, 8 ft.

109. **Bog Willow.** *Salix pedicellaris.* Shrub, 3 ft.

110. **Bebb Willow.** *Salix bebbiana.* Small tree, 15 ft.

111. **Purpleosier.** *Salix purpurea.* Small tree, 15 ft. Polished olive-colored branches.

112. **Silky Willow.** *Salix rigida.* Shrub, 15 ft.

113. **American Chestnut.** *Castanea dentata.* Tree, 100 ft. 3 sweet nuts in a bur; bark, dark lead-gray.

114. **American Beech.** *Fagus grandifolia.* Tree, 70 ft. 2 triangular nuts in each bur; bark light gray, smooth.

115. **American Basswood.** *Tilia americana.* Tree, 50 ft. Yellowish-white fragrant flowers borne in clusters on large leafy bracts.

116. **Witch-Hazel.** *Hamamelis virginiana.* Shrub, 20 ft. The yellow flowers with long straplike petals appear in late autumn after leaves have fallen.

117. **Red Mulberry.** *Morus rubra.* Tree, 30 ft. Dark purple, blackberry-like fruits.

118. **Hackberry.** *Celtis occidentalis.* Tree, 40 ft. Sweet cherry-like fruits.

119. **European Buckthorn.** *Rhamnus cathartica.* Small tree, 20 ft. The small black fleshy fruits, borne in clusters, have purgative properties.

120. **Alder Buckthorn.** *Rhamnus alnifolia.* Shrub, 3 ft. Black pear-shaped berries with 3 seeds.

121. **American Holly.** *Ilex opaca.* Tree, 20 ft. Flowers white, bright scarlet-red berries.

122. **Mountain Holly.** *Nemopanthus mucronata.* Shrub, 10 ft. Beautiful pale crimson berries on long red stems.

123. **Winterberry.** *Ilex verticellata.* Shrub, 10 ft. Bright red berries on short stems, scattered on branches.

124. **Smooth Winterberry.** *Ilex laevigata.* Shrub, 10 ft. Orange-red berries on very short stems.

125. **Inkberry.** *Ilex glabra.* Shrub, 6 ft. Evergreen, white flowers and black berries.

126. **New Jersey Tea.** *Ceanothus americanus.* Shrub, 3 ft. Flowers white, in clusters on white stems.

127. **Sweet Pepperbush.** *Clethra alnifolia.* Shrub, 6 ft. White fragrant flowers, late in August.

128. **Bittersweet.** *Celastrus scandens.* Vine. Fruit a thin, 3-valved globular pod containing 3 seeds covered with a crimson aril, the open fruit and seeds persistent into the early winter.

129. **Sweet Gale.** *Myrica gale.* Shrub, 4 ft. A dark bush, growing in patches in swamps.

130. **Wax Myrtle.** *Myrica cerifera.* Shrub, 7 ft. Leaves and berries with balsamic odor.

131. **Common Barberry.** *Berberis vulgaris.* Shrub, 6 ft. Flowers yellow; fruit long oval, orange, fleshy; twigs with branched spines; wood yellow.

132. **Downy Serviceberry.** *Amelanchier arborea.* Shrub, or small tree, 15 ft. Pear-shaped purplish berries, sweet.

133. **Chokeberry.** *Aronia arbutifolia.* Shrub, 5 ft. Reddish-purple, dry astringent fruit.

134. **American Plum.** *Prunus americana.* Tree, 15 ft. Reddish-orange astringent plum.

135. **Beach Plum.** *Prunus maritima.* Shrub, 4 ft. Plum globular, purple.

136. **Sloe.** *Prunus spinosa.* Tree, 15 ft. Plum round, black, with yellowish bloom.

137. **Pin Cherry.** *Prunus pensylvania.* Tree, 15 ft. Small, sour, red cherries.

138. **Sand Cherry.** *Prunus pumila.* Trailing, 1 ft. Dark red cherries; edible.

139. **Black Cherry.** *Prunus serotina.* Tree, 40 ft. Black-purplish, aromatic cherries.

140. **Choke Cherry.** *Prunus virginiana.* Tree, 10 ft. Dark red, pleasant, but bitter cherries.

141. **Possumhaw Viburnum.** *Viburnum nudum.* Shrub, 10 ft. Fruit fleshy, dark blue.

142. **Nannyberry Viburnum.** *Viburnum lentago.* Shrub, 15 ft. Fruit fleshy, dark scarlet colored.

143. **Arrowwood Viburnum.** *Viburnum dentatum.* Shrub, 10 ft. Fruit fleshy, dark blue-lead colored.

144. **Mapleleaf Viburnum.** *Viburnum acerifolium.* Shrub, 6 ft. Fleshy fruits blue-black.

145. **American Cranberrybush.** *Viburnum trilobum.* Shrub, 10 ft. Fruit fleshy, red, pleasantly acidulous.

146. **Wayfaringtree.** *Viburnum lantana.* Shrub, 20 ft. Fruit fleshy, egg-shaped, dark red.

147. **Bush Honeysuckle.** *Diervilla lonicera.* Shrub, 4 ft. Flowers yellow.

148. **Common Greenbrier.** *Smilax rotundifolia.* Thorny vine, green stem, blue-black berries.

149. **Carrion Flower Greenbrier.** *Smilax herbacea.* Vine. Not thorny, flowers exhaling a fetid odor.

150. **Persimmon.** *Diospyros virginiana.* Tree, 30 ft. Plumlike, fruit edible after frost.

151. **Black Tupelo.** *Nyssa sylvatica.* Tree, 30 ft. Horizontal branches, blue berries.

152. **Spicebush.** *Lindera benzoin.* Shrub, 10 ft. Flowers yellow, fruit fleshy, red, leaves fragrant.

153. **Rhodora.** *Azalea canadensis.* Shrub, 5 ft. Flower purple-rose colored.

154. **Clammy Azalea.** *Azalea viscosa.* Shrub, 8 ft. White fragrant flowers.

155. **Pink Azalea.** *Azalea nudiflora.* Shrub, 5 ft. Dark red fragrant flowers, appearing before leaves.

156. **Leatherwood.** *Dirca palustris.* Shrub, 5 ft. Bark very tough, stem swollen at the nodes.

157. **Staggerbush.** *Leucothoe racemosa.* Shrub, 6 ft. White flower, cylindrical bell-shaped.

158. **Maleberry.** *Andromeda ligustrina.* Shrub, 8 ft. Flowers white, bell-shaped.

159. **Highbush Blueberry.** *Vaccinium corymbosum.*
     (a) var. *glabrum,* smooth leaves with entire margins.
     (b) var. *amoenum,* bristly leaves with serrate margins.
     (c) var. *atrococcum,* woolly leaves and black fruit.

160. **Pinweeds.** *Lechea* spp. Heath-like bushes, 1 ft. Purple-brown flowers.

161. **Frostweed.** *Helianthemum canadense.* 1 ft. Flower yellow.

162. **Blueridge Blueberry.** *Vaccinium pallidum.* Shrub, 2 ft. Late blueberry.

163. **Low Sweet Blueberry.** *Vaccinium angustifolium.* Shrub, 1 ft. Earliest blueberry; also a black variety.

164. **Black Huckleberry.** *Gaylussacia baccata.* Shrub, 2 ft. Berries shining black, sweet; leaves glandular below.

165. **Dangleberry.** *Gaylussacia frondosa.* Shrub, 5 ft. Berries large, blue on slender stem; acidulous.

166. **Dwarf Huckleberry.** *Gaylussacia dumosa.* Shrub, 2 ft. Berries large, black, tasteless.

167. **Deerberry.** *Vaccinium stamineum.* Shrub, 3 ft. Berries greenish-white. Not edible.

168. **Beechheathers.** *Hudsonia* spp. Heath-like sand plants, 6 in., of gray aspect; flowers yellow.

169. **Rosebay Rhododendron.** *Rhododendron maximum.* Shrub, 7 ft. Flowers pale rose color.

170. **Sweetbay.** *Magnolia virginiana.* Shrub, 8 ft. Flowers large, white.

171. **Mountain-Laurel.** *Kalmia latifolia.* Shrub, 8 ft. Flowers white, and pinkish-white.

172. **Sheep-Laurel.** *Kalmia angustifolia.* Shrub, 2 ft. Flowers deep rose-red; leaves in 3's.

174. **Labrador Tea.** *Ledum groenlandicum.* Shrub, 3 ft. Flowers white, leaves rusty-woolly below.

175. **Large Cranberry.** *Vaccinium macrocarpum.* Shrub, 2 ft. Berries large, bright scarlet-red.

176. **Small Cranberry.** *Vaccinium oxycoccos.* Plant, 1/2 ft. Berries red, small.

177. **Leatherleaf.** *Chamaedaphne calyculata.* Shrub, 3 ft. Flowers white, grows in patches in meadows.

178. **Broom Crowberry.** *Cormea conradii.* Shrub, 2 ft. Flowers purple, heath-like plant.

179. **Bog-Rosemary.** *Andromeda polifolia.* Shrub, 1 ft. Flowers snow-white or flesh colored.

180. **Cowberry.** *Vaccinium vitis-idaea.* Shrub, 6 in. Creeping; berries dark-red, bitter.

181. **Pipsissewa.** *Chimaphila umbellata.* Plant, 6 in. Flower flesh colored.

182. **Spotted wintergreen.** *Chimaphila maculata.* Plant, 4 in. Leaves spotted with white.

183. **Teaberry.** *Gaultheria procumbens.* Plant, 4 in. Berries red, and leaves spicy.

184. **Pyrolas.** *Pyrola* spp. Low-creeping evergreens. Flower stems, 8 in. Flowers pale greenish-white.

185. **Bearberry.** *Arctostaphylos uva-ursi.* Trailing plant, on rocks. Leaves thick, berries red.

186. **Creeping Pearlberry.** *Chiogenes hispidula.* Creeping plant with white berries. Edible.

187. **Trailing Arbutus.** *Epigaea repens.* Creeping. Flowers rose colored, or pearly white, fragrant.

188. **Bunchberry.** *Cornus canadensis.* Plant, 6 in. Flowers white, berries red, in bunches.

189. **Flowering Dogwood.** *Cornus florida.* Tree, 10 to 30 ft. Flowers white, berries bright scarlet.

190. **Roundleaf Dogwood.** *Cornus rugosa.* Shrub, 6 to 10 ft. Flowers white, berries blue, turning whitish.

191. **Red-Osier Dogwood.** *Cornus stolonifera.* Shrub, 3 to 6 ft. Blood red stems, fruit white, or lead colored.

192. **Panicled Dogwood.** *Cornus paniculata.* Shrub, 4 to 8 ft. Flowers white, berries round, pale white.

193. **Alternateleaf Dogwood.** *Cornus alternifolia.* Shrub 8 to 20 ft. Flowers pale yellowish-white, berries blue-black.

194. **Silky Dogwood.** *Cornus amomum.* Shrub, 3 to 10 ft. Flowers white inside, yellow outside.

195. **Privet.** *Ligustrum vulgare.* Shrub, 8 ft. Flowers white, berries shining black.

196. **Buttonbush.** *Cephalanthus occidentalis.* Shrub, 10 ft. Flowers in yellowish-white balls.

197. **American Fly Honeysuckle.** *Lonicera canadensis.* Shrub, 5 ft. Flowers greenish-yellow, fruit fleshy, red.

198. **Sweetberry Honeysuckle.** *Lonicera coerulea.* Shrub, 3 ft. Flowers yellow, berries blue.

199. **Common Horsegentian.** *Triosteum perfoliatum.* Shrub, 3 ft. Flowers purple, in clusters, berries orange.

200. **Limber Honeysuckle.** *Lonicera dioica.* Vine. Yellow tinged purple flowers, berries orange.

201. **Hairy Honeysuckle.** *Lonicera hirsuta.* Vine. Flowers pale yellow outside, rich orange inside, berries orange.

202. **Twinflower.** *Linnaea borealis.* Creeping. Flowers in 2's, white and rose-tinted; fruit dry.

203. **Partridgeberry.** *Mitchella repens.* Creeping. Flowers in 2's, white or rose colored, fragrant, scarlet berries.

204. **Tamarack.** *Larix laricina.* Tree, 70 ft. Cones 1/2 in. long; bark bluish-gray.

205. **Red Pine.** *Pinus resinosa.* Tree, 70 ft. Bark reddish, rather smooth; cones 2 in. long, in clusters, not prickly.

206. **Pitch Pine.** *Pinus rigida.* Tree, 60 ft. Very rough, dark bark; very pitchy cones, 2 in. long, prickly.

207. **Eastern White Pine.** *Pinus strobus.* Tree, 150 ft. Bark smooth, cones 5 in. long, not prickly, brittle, soft, white wood.

208. **Balsam Fir.** *Abies balsamea.* Tree, 40 ft. Cones 3 in. long, standing erect on the limbs.

209. **Black Spruce.** *Picea mariana.* Tree, 50 ft. Cones 1 in. long, hanging downwards from limb.

210. **Eastern Hemlock** *Tsuga canadensis.* Tree, 70 ft. Cones 1/2 in. long; most graceful tree when young; poor wood, very knotty, hard.

211. **Northern White-cedar.** *Thuja occidentalis.* Tree, 40 ft. Cones small, 1/2 in. long.

212. **Atlantic White-Cedar.** *Chamaecyparis thyoides.* Tree, 60 ft. Cones as large as peas. In swamps.

213. **Eastern Redcedar.** *Juniperus virginiana.* Tree, 30 ft. Wood red, fragrant; cones fleshy, blue.

214. **Common Juniper.** *Juniperus communis.* Spreading shrub, 2 ft. Dark purple fleshy cones.

215. **Canada Yew.** *Taxus canadensis.* Low, straggling bush. Seed enveloped in a red, resinous aril.